# Planets

by Martha E. H. Rustad

**CAPSTONE PRESS**
a capstone imprint

Little Pebble is published by Capstone Press,
1710 Roe Crest Drive, North Mankato, Minnesota 56003
www.capstonepub.com

**Library of Congress Cataloging-in-Publication Data**
Rustad, Martha E. H. (Martha Elizabeth Hillman), 1975– author.
  Planets / by Martha E. H. Rustad.
      pages cm. — (Little pebble. Space)
  Audience: Ages 5–7.
  Audience: K to grade 3.
  Summary: "Simple text and full-color photographs describe the planets"—Provided by
the publisher.
  Includes bibliographical references and index.
  ISBN 978-1-4914-8322-0 (library binding)
  ISBN 978-1-4914-8326-8 (paperback)
  ISBN 978-1-4914-8330-5 (eBook PDF)
  1.  Planets—Juvenile literature. 2.  Solar system—Juvenile literature. I. Title.
  QB602.R86 2016
  523.2—dc23                                                                2015023308

**Editorial Credits**
Erika L. Shores, editor; Juliette Peters and Katelin Plekkenpol, designers;
Tracy Cummins, media researcher; Katy LaVigne, production specialist

**Photo Credits**
NASA: JPL, 17; Science Source: SPL, 11, 21; Shutterstock: cigdem, 15, Kalenik Hanna, Design
Element, manjik, 9, Michelangelus, 7, Tristan3D, 19, Vadim Sadovski, 13, Thinkstock: rwarnick,
cover, 1; Wikimedia: NASA/GSFC/NOAA/USGS, 5

**Editor's Note**
In this book's photographs, the sizes of objects and the distances between them
are not to scale.

Printed and bound in China.
007475LEOS16

# Table of Contents

# Home, Sweet Home!

We live on Earth.

It is a planet.

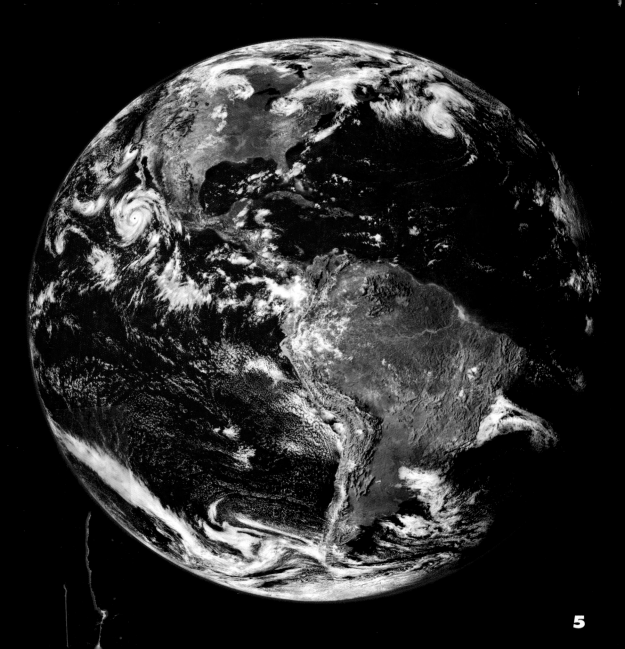

Planets orbit stars.

The sun is a star.

The sun has eight planets.

Earth is one of them.

# Close to the Sun!

Mercury and Venus are

close to the sun.

Mars and Earth are too.

**Mercury**

**Venus**

**Earth**

**Mars**

They are called
the inner planets.
They are rocky.

Mercury

# Far Away!

Jupiter and Saturn are far
from the sun.
Uranus and Neptune are too.

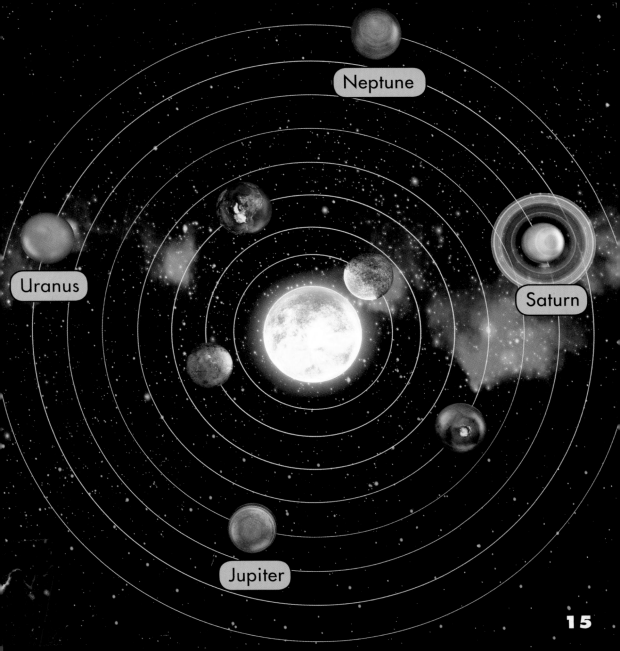

Neptune

Uranus

Saturn

Jupiter

They are called

the outer planets.

They are made of gas.

Neptune

Uranus

Saturn

Jupiter

The outer planets are big.
Jupiter is as big as
1,300 Earths.

Earth

Jupiter

Look up. See the night sky.

You can spot some planets!

Saturn

Mars

Venus

Mercury

# Glossary

**gas**—a substance that spreads to fill any space that holds it

**orbit**—to follow a curved path around an object in space

**planet**—a large object in space that orbits a star

**star**—a ball of burning gases

# Read More

**DeYoe, Aaron.** *Planets.* Out of This World. Minneapolis: Abdo Publishing, 2016.

**Mapua, Jeff.** *What Is a Planet?* Let's Find Out! Space. New York: Britannica Educational Publishing with Rosen Educational Services, 2015.

**Simon, Seymour.** *Our Solar System.* New York: HarperCollins Publishers, 2014.

# Internet Sites

FactHound offers a safe, fun way to find Internet sites related to this book. All of the sites on FactHound have been researched by our staff.

Here's all you do:
Visit *www.facthound.com*
Type in this code: 9781491483220

 Check out projects, games and lots more at
**www.capstonekids.com**

# Index